Hope

Saved Me

"I have hated everyone all my life and now I hate no one"

Contents

Foreword 4

Acknowledgements...5

Pastor's Foreword 7

Special Thanks..9

I Lived In Fear 10

"I Really Wanted What Billy Had"............................... 14

Something Greater Than I Could Even Imagine 18

You Are Only As Sick As Your Secrets 20

Hakuna Matata.. 22

I Will Restore To You the Years That the Locust Has Eaten 25

God Took Me Up On My Offer 28

Fence Talks... 35

Tighty Whittie... 38

"That's for you, it's not for me!" 40

Albert Was the Main Reason 42

Not Real Heart Questions 44

Painful To Hear His Venom.. 46

Randy and Rod Never Gave Up! 48

This Was In No Way a Shock to God 51

His First Real Heart Questions..56

I Was Enabling Him 59

This Hurt My Heart Deeply 63

Biggest Conflict We Ever Had...66

Face Down In the Grass..68

Heap Burning Coals on His Head 70

He Would Listen Intently...72

She and Others in the Community Had Been Praying For Albert ...74

Three Days Crying Out To Jesus 77

Whose Heart Was Like a Child...81

Toenail clipper...83

He Was Mad 86

Church Erupted With Cheering...90

Whole Story Complete..93

It's Your Fault 95

He Wanted To Be At His New Address...97

Imaginings of the Future He Wouldn't Have 102

Nursing Home or Face Legal Issues..103

Just In The Nick Of Time 104

93-Year-Old Frenchman 106

Foreword

Robert Frost once said "Good fences make good neighbors." But what would happen if there were no fences and we each entered our neighbors' lives- loving them as we love ourselves? This is the story of one man who determined to tear down the fence piece by piece in an effort to serve and love his neighbor. But Albert didn't make it easy. Albert was a 90-year-old Frenchman, abandoned at birth on an orphanage doorstep. He was a veteran, a painter and a chef; however, he was also divorced, alone, angry and bitter. But Tim determined to love him no matter what. That relationship grew from daily fence talks to caring intimately for Albert in his final days. Ultimately this is a story of the radical transformation that can occur when we become not just neighbors but the hands and feet of Jesus. And that transformation wasn't just Albert's transformation and redemption. When we serve others, God ultimately changes us. In our service we are often given a glimpse of God's love for us. This story is for anyone that has ever been challenged with a difficult relationship or anyone that has ever felt their life could not be redeemed. This is a story of redemption literally in the nick of time!

Whatever you did for one of the least of these brothers and sisters of mine, you did it to me.

Matthew 25:40.

Marie Cadden

Acknowledgements

I want to thank Pastor Rod Addison for planting the first seeds about writing this story. I must admit upon hearing him recommend this, I laughed inside. The laughter soon disappeared and changed to something that captured my complete attention as Rod later shared about telling some fellow pastors about Albert and our friendship. He said they were so amazed by the story that they asked him if they could share with their own congregations. It soon became clear to me that I was receiving a push that I knew from experience was God's hand. Thank you Rod for this encouragement and your steady guiding hand in my life!

I want to thank Kim Hartenstein. Kim is the Administrative Assistant and Lead Technical Adviser at West Town Community Church. Her truest title is "God's Assistant." Kim will do anything she can to serve the Lord. She volunteered to do the typing of my handwritten account of Albert's story. Volunteered is not the description of what she really did. She actually requested to do this because she felt led to be a part of making all this happen. To fully understand how daunting this task would be, I must point out that she had to be able to read my handwriting! This was akin to reading a foreign language for the first time. She never complained! On top of that she and her husband Fred just took on the task of raising four young children in the middle of this. Thank you, Kim!

I also want to thank Dawn Gonzalez who accepted the mountainous task of being the main editor of this book. I remember her profound words that she said when she described what she wanted to accomplish. She said, "I want to do this for the reader so that it is easy for them to read and grasp what is being said and told." That is my paraphrase but its close. I wanted to say to her laughingly "Good luck with that." I was handing her a very tough task because of my lack of skill as a writer. I was so overwhelmed when I read the story for the first time after she had worked her magic. Thank you, Dawn! You are amazing.

Lastly, I want to thank Marie Cadden. As you read this book you will see why it is only appropriate that the Cadden name and fingerprints would be in this page as well. Marie Cadden, you have been so instrumental in the final stages for all of the editing and writing of the book description. You captured the whole meaning in this book in such a concise way. You and your entire family have blessed me and my family for so many years! Thank you.

Pastor's Foreword

Greetings! I am delighted that you have picked this book up. You will not regret it!

I had a front row seat as the events in this book unfolded. Sometimes I found myself relaxed, other times frustrated, but mostly on the edge of my seat.

The two main characters in this story could not have been more different. Albert was a crusty cantankerous and bitter old man who wore these feelings on his sleeves. Tim, in contrast, is a gentle, kind, loving, God-fearing, Jesus-following man, humble and strong.

The thread that wove the patches of this tattered relationship into something beautiful was the gentle work of the Holy Spirit. If you are skeptic, a cynic, or a believer you have probably asked the question, "How does God work in this world?" This story is a heart-warming example of how God works to soften a hard heart. It also shows the many ways God works to orchestrate the details of our life to have us at the right place doing the right thing at the right time. Sit back, fasten your seat belt, and grab some popcorn and a drink. You are about to experience a firsthand story that you will not soon forget.

I serve as Tim's pastor and have watched God do a mighty work in his life which has had a deep impact on his children, his church family, his work place and his neighborhood.

I had the privilege of being Albert's pastor for the last few months of his life.

The story you are about to read will inspire you to live for God's highest purpose even in the routine day to day activities. God is always at work around us, we just have to see what God sees. More often than not our opportunity is right in front of us.

Happy reading!

Pastor Rod Addison

Special Thanks

I want to give special thanks to my children, children in law, and grandchildren. To my children I want to say with all my heart thank you for giving me your forgiveness and for giving me a second chance at being your father. Your complete forgiveness overwhelms me! It has been such a beautiful journey watching each of you come to know Christ personally and seeing you become the person He intended for you to be. You are beautiful pictures of Christ's work in your lives. Thank you for giving me the best seat in the house to watch your stories. Tyler, Sierra, and Ellie I am the most blessed man on this planet to be your father!

Drew and Taylor, my children in law, I have said this to you both. You are more than I could have ever imagined. You are both so gifted in so many ways, but your greatest gift is your love for the Lord and others.

To my four grandchildren Preston, Bentley, Tatum & Cadden, as well as Everett Wayne Patrick soon to be born this October, I am so thankful that I got picked to be your Pops. I love our many adventures but what I love most is the opportunity to see what God is doing in each of your lives. What an adventure that is!!

Psalms 128 Vs. 3 "...Your children shall be like olive plants around your table."

Psalms 128 Vs. 6 "...Indeed, may you live to see your children's children."

9

I Lived In Fear

This is a book to honor the promise I made to my dear friend Albert Glaicz. It's a story of hope for Albert, but to tell his story, I must begin with my own. I grew up in the country, known by some as the boondocks. I lived on 40 acres of farm land with a garden and cows and pigs. I grew up in a pretty big family with three brothers and two sisters. My dad, a WWII veteran, participated in major battles during the war. He had many stories of his time there, including the day he stormed the shores at the Normandy Invasion, landing on Utah beach for D-day. These experiences made him as tough as they come, and he ruled over the home with an iron fist of a temper. My brothers and I used to laugh as adults about the fact that that Dad would use a switch when he disciplined us and his discipline would be done in white hot anger, we would say "he would switch us until he felt better". We deserved every switching we got but Dad's inability to show us love or ever tell us he loved us, left damage in each of our hearts that would take years to reconcile within us. He did not let that tough exterior down long enough to ever tell me and my siblings that he loved us when we were growing up. My dad was not a Christian and he was doing just as his dad had modeled. But our mom was much the opposite of him being full of love, always caring for us, and even was our protector many times when dad would lose his temper. My brothers and I all became brawlers at home and with our classmates, and, because I wanted to be like them, I began to fight as well. I had a growing anger within me that would manifest itself in this outburst of fighting. Things were almost always chaotic at home which seemed to always translate to chaos at school too. I remember once seeing my oldest brother get into a fight with my Dad and now that he was bigger and stronger than my Dad, he held him down on the floor and beat him with a belt buckle. It was a terrifying sight for anyone to see, but especially an 8-year-old boy.

It was the 70s, when things were changing in ways I could not quite understand at that young age. There were riots in the streets, the Vietnam War was unfolding, and desegregation was all taking place. The volatility at home, at school, and in society impacting much of my childhood. I was in the eighth grade when I was a part of the first group of students in Aiken, South Carolina to be transferred to an all-Black school in order to begin integration in my area. That began an endless cycle of campus fights and police enforcement of all the violence that was going on. I lived in fear at school and at home with my dad and brothers, and I became a very introverted person growing up.

We attended church on occasion but outside of that my parents never spoke about God except for saying a memorized blessing before we ate. The one thing that did impact me at this young of an age is that the men of the church would have camping trips to various places like the mountains or several ponds that our men owned. It was here that I would see different examples of men that really spoke to me. They were joyful and interested in us boys and obviously wanted to give their time to invest in us. I thank the Lord for them all to this day. If I tried to name them all I am afraid I would omit someone so I will just say with all my heart thank you. You all made a difference in my life!!

When I got older, I got my first job plowing fields with a tractor for my cousin who was much older than me for $1.00 per hour. I would do 12-hour days of hard labor, and to this day I have deep respect for farmers who work harder than many. This job led to another job that I thought better suited me at the cotton mill. There I worked six days a week, eight hours a day from 4:00 P.M. to midnight after attending full days of high school. I did not study at all, and I slept through the first few periods of school every day.

I was introduced to drinking and weed by this time and the immediate attraction that I had was overwhelming. In short it made me feel different, and I did not want to feel the way I had been feeling for years. By the time I reached my senior year I did not attend school unless I was high, because it was not worth it without the drugs in my system. Weed was the only thing that made life worth living and allowed me to escape the difficult and painful parts of my life. . It was my sole joy in life, so I smoked as much as possible.

I was a troubled teenager, working a full-time job of physical labor and at night, taking drugs and abusing alcohol. I also embraced the 1970s "free love" movement that was infiltrating culture at the time. This unsustainable lifestyle eventually came crashing down on me. I was arrested for possession of marijuana. In fact, I had to be arrested twice within six-months in order for the Lord to shake me awake. The second arrest happened on my high school campus after I had turned 17, meaning I was no longer a juvenile. I was expelled from school, and it was highly possible that I would be sent to a "youth correction camp" to reform me. I was terrified.

"I Really Wanted What Billy Had"

The next day, suddenly, these charges disappeared. I was not going to jail! It seemed like things began to look up, things that still to this day I cannot explain, other than God was intervening in my life.

That next Sunday I got myself to church no matter what. I felt like I needed to after all of this. While I was at church that Sunday, a man about eight years older than me named Billy Eubanks came up to me. He said, "I know what happened to you, if you will go to school, I want to pay your tuition at a private school." Billy was the coach of our church's softball team and he was an amazing Christlike example. So, when he made his request, I was skeptical and filled with doubt. I thought *if he really knows who I am and what happened to me, why in the world would he throw money away on me?* I just kept replaying his words in my head wondering why, and how this be could be happening.

I began thinking this was the Lord telling me I have reached a crossroads. I finally had the chance to get out of the life I was living and choose a different road. This brought me to my knees. I cried and pleaded and wondered. How could I give up this life and my friends? But also, how could I give up this opportunity? I knew deep down what I really wanted was what Billy had, so I finally let go and asked God to please "give *me what Billy had.*"

In that moment it felt like the weight of the world was lifted off my shoulders, and I wanted everyone to know it. I called my best friend and told him what happened to me and asked him to go to church with me so he could experience it, too. He declined my offer and was not very pleased when I told him I would not be living in the same way I had been before, which was the foundation of our friendship. I then thought that I needed to tell my parents that everything was about to change for me. When I was sitting there recounting to them the events that had just taken place and telling them that my whole life was about to look different, they sat there wide-eyed and confused. Of course they responded as most parents would, with encouragement, but really, they did not expect anything to be different, as I was, a few days prior, a very irresponsible and troubled teenager. My next decision was to be baptized, so I went to my pastor. He dunked me in order that I could proclaim that I had truly allowed Christ to have control of my life and share this with my friends and family.

I finally went back to school the following fall, but this time with a work ethic I had never had before. I wanted to make up for the lost time of my past so I took classes that would challenge me like Chemistry and other classes that I never would have attempted before. However, to my dismay, being a new follower of Christ did not mean I suddenly knew all the things I should have learned in school but didn't. Even though school was hard and I was not suddenly an all-star student, there were wonderful things happening in my life spiritually. My two oldest brothers became followers of Christ. Then one of the most amazing things of all happened. I received a call from my Dad at my college around 6:30 one morning. My Dad was on the phone crying hysterically. I was in a bit of shock because I had never seen him like this before. I asked him a series of questions like what had happened, Dad are you alright? Is mom alright? Has something happened to any of the children? He told me no and said just give him a moment so he could collect himself and he would tell me. I listened as he continued crying in the background as my stomach was in a knot. Finally, he began to speak, and these are the words he said to me. He said, "I went to church yesterday and the preacher said, for a man to become a Christian he must be born again. He said," I could not stop thinking about those words all night and I felt so burdened in my heart that I called into work and asked off for the day. "He said "I got on my knees beside my bed and I said to God I will not get up from here until I know that I am Born Again. He said I asked the Lord to forgive me and come into my heart. Then he said in a loud voice crying out, I know I am Born Again. Then he said, "I love you!" My heart felt as though it flew out of my chest with joy.

In the years to come I watched his life change in magnificent ways. He talked to me about the beatings and explained how he had learned that from his father and that he was so sorry. I forgave him and watched him over the years become a loving gentle man that cried and prayed with me when I had problems. Later, he was even ordained as a deacon in our home church. In the last years of my Dad's life he became my best friend and I will forever cherish the healing time we had together. This event as well as many relationships with my classmates like my good friend Jack Folk and other classmates who told me that they had decided to follow Christ and shared that it was through my life changing that he saw Christ's supreme worth. I remember thinking that I had unknowingly become their "Billy" in their lives, as Billy had in mine. It brought me such joy to know God was using me to bring others into a relationship with Christ. Even more amazing was the fact that most of the time I was totally unaware that God was doing this.

Something Greater Than I Could Even Imagine

I began to sense something much deeper working in my heart and life. I could not shake the feeling that the Lord was calling me to something greater than I could even imagine. All I knew is that my life was not going to be fulfilled doing anything other than what he asked of me. I decided to share this with my pastor, Dan Johnston who has been an amazing influence in my life and still is to this very day. Pastor Johnston said I am going to take you to Anderson College to be trained in the ministry. That sounded like the most impossible thing I had ever heard. What college would ever allow me to attend their school?

To my surprise and shock, they accepted me into the college, and I was scared out of my mind. After all, I had an arrest record, and was expelled from high school. I went back to finished high school and ended up being ranked 582nd out of 635 in my class. The surprising part to me was not how low I ranked, but the fact that I beat 53 other people. So, I began college at Anderson Junior College and cautiously, I began to consider myself college material.

With some fear of failing as motivation, I began to study, working harder than I ever knew I could, and I began to think that I just might make it. I was asked to be the speaker on what my college called the Deputation Team. The college provided us use of their van on the weekends to travel to speak, sing, and do church services on weekends. We saw some wonderful things done by the Lord in those services, and I will never forget those experiences. After one of these services at Bounty Land Baptist Church, they asked me if I would be their summer youth minister. I accepted and served there for the next three summers.

As I began to wrap up college, I felt led to go to Southwestern Baptist Theological Seminary in Fort Worth TX. I was accepted into the seminary and spent the next three and a half years getting my Masters of Divinity. After graduation, I served as youth minister at a church in Spartanburg, South Carolina and was ordained by the leaders in that church.

You Are Only As Sick As Your Secrets

While all of this was an amazing experience and I was able to learn and grow and follow where I felt the Lord was leading me, I also struggled harder than ever in my walk with the Lord in these later years. I struggled with deep sin in my life that I began to take less seriously, and I began to fall more often. This caused my relationship with the Lord to grow increasingly distant as time went on. My conscience was seared, and I lost touch with who God had called me to be.

It was not long after becoming the youth pastor in Spartanburg that I began to reap what I was sowing in my sin. I was out of control in the area of sexual sin, and instead of seeking help, I hid it.

I once heard a good friend of mine say, "You are only as sick as your secrets." I had never learned the importance of walking with other Christians in an accountable relationship because I was afraid that this would cost me the ministry I had prepared for, but the very opposite was true. What was going to cost me the ministry was *not* letting someone who maybe could have helped me know.

I married and had a son named Tyler, and my marriage lasted only two years. I had to leave the new church I was in, and suddenly I realized life was going to be much different than I had hoped for. It was more than I could handle, and I did not want to face any of my problems. I had a 2-year-old son, and I was going through a divorce.

I wanted to forget all the destruction in my past and all the pain that I had caused for other people, so instead of getting help from someone and turning back to God, I fell even deeper into it. I again turned to alcohol to ease my pain. I worked hard to sedate myself trying not to feel the pain and suffering going on. But ironically, even giving my best effort, I could not forget the most painful part of it all. I constantly was aware of the pain of being so far from God, not having a daily relationship with him.

I ended up remarrying during all this and had two beautiful daughters Sierra and Ellie. I went into the sales industry and drank every single day for the next 25 years.

Hakuna Matata

When I had given up on the possibility of ever getting things right with God, I noticed something happening on a semi-regular basis. I would wake up in the middle of the night and sense God speaking to me. I sensed it not with my ears but with my heart. It was not harsh words like "you filthy drunk, why don't you get your stinking life together," It was, instead, words of invitation: "I miss our time together," and "I love you." I would literally flip over to my other side and say, "Not now God, I don't want to talk." Then one Night I had the most vivid dream I have ever had that started a chain of events that would bring me to the end of myself and the beginning of a brand-new life.

I dreamt that I was seeing the movie *The Lion King*, and while I was watching it God was using all the words in the movie to speak to me. It was the scene where lion named Simba, who had been living with the Meerkat and Warthog and eating grub worms while singing Hakuna Matata, No Worries. Simba began talking to Rafiki, the monkey. Rafiki tells Simba his dad who was killed, is still alive. Simba runs to see if this is true and thinks he is tricked by Rafiki but then realizes the truth, that his dad is alive, 'in him'. Then the words rain down, "Remember who you are." I woke up and gasped for breath. God was simply reminding me to remember who I am. Reminding me that I was still His child and that cannot be changed. It was Him calling me back to who I am. A man who is as broken as can be, but still the man He gave his Son's life to purchase me, and He had not changed His mind about loving me. He could not be unfaithful to me; it is not who He is. When I got up that morning I was shaking, I called my Pastor Rod Addison and said I needed to talk.

We met at a restaurant and I told him in tears what had happened. He did his best to help me but I still was not ready. I was going to church sporadically only so my daughters could hear and learn about Christ, when the final blow came. I was at Edisto Beach State Park on a camping trip with my wife, daughters, and other extended family. I got so drunk I did not remember how I got back to my tent. In the middle of the night I had to use the bathroom and tried to unzip the tent only to fall all over on everyone and into the sides of the tent. I looked over and saw my daughter Sierra hiding behind her mother in fear of me. She had never seen me this drunk and she was in fear of what I might do.

For the rest of the weekend I could not get Sierra's eyes of fear looking at me out of my mind. The same eyes that once said, "If someone were to try to harm me, my dad would die to protect me," were now uncertain eyes, wondering if I would be the one to harm her.

My brother Troy also got drunk that night, as I did, and as we drove to our respective home in separate cars, we both cried out to God, not knowing that the other one was doing the same. My prayer went something like this, "God, enough is enough. I am sorry for all my sins, and I will do anything you ask. I will let go of everything.

Change me and create in me a clean heart." I wept like a child, but I knew everything was going to change.

I Will Restore To You the Years That the Locust Has Eaten

Joel 2 :25 KJV

I had never led my children for a single day as an example of a man walking with God, and I now intended to finish this race I started over 40 years ago. I prayed this to God, "My first two kids are almost grown and out of the home and I cannot make up for the lost time. I bring them to you, and I give them all to you including Ellie who was now about 5 years old. Raise them up for your glory even if it means they die for their faith. They are yours now. Use me in any way you decide as an example of who you are."

As I began this journey again with Christ, there were several verses that I loved and asked God to bring about in my life and the life of my family. One verse was Joel 2:25, "So I will restore to you the years that the locust has eaten away." Another verse was Jeremiah 29:11, "For I know the plans I have for you," declares the Lord, "plans to prosper you and not to harm you, plans to give you hope and a future." And the verse in Isaiah 44:5, " still others will write on their hands, "Belonging to the Lord" and will take the name Israel.

All of these verses were centered on asking God to transform me and my family. I shared Isaiah 44:5 with my children and my daughter Sierra made a picture of her, Tyler, my son, and Ellie, my other daughter, holding their hands up chest high with the words written on them, "Belonging to God." She had not even come to Christ yet, but she understood my desire for her and her siblings. They gave this picture to me as a birthday present, and I wept like a baby again.

Mike Hullum, My second sponsor

I immersed myself in Celebrate Recovery to work through the temptations of alcohol and sexual sin. My pastor walked with me anytime I would lose my balance spiritually, as did Bob Kingdom and Mike Hullum, my first and second sponsors respectively and other men in my church who came along beside me like Charlie Bearden, Dave Cadden, Dave Perry, Drew Pie, Tom Duke and so many others including my own children who became great encouragers to me. I also was encouraged greatly by the Godly ladies in our church who were a constant source of love. I was finding success because of these surrounding me and I was no longer willing to be as sick as my secrets, like an old friend once wisely warned.

From left to right Bob Kingdom, my first sponsor in Celebrate Recovery, me, Charlie Bearden- a brother in Christ that has walked with me for 11 years

The picture that Sierra gave me for my birthday

God Took Me Up On My Offer

It seemed I was changing daily and God would use His peace to be His guiding force. If I did not have peace about something, I would take a step backwards. There were other things that I felt God speaking to my heart about as well. I remember during the first few months of my recovery sitting in my house and thinking back over all that I had worked and strived for the last 20 years. It embarrassed and saddened me. I spent all that time working to buy a nice house and provide materially and no time being my family's spiritual example of what it looked like to walk with Christ. I cried and prayed, "God I am sorry. You can have it all." Little did I know it would soon be gone in the divorce settlement. God took me up on my offer.

I moved into a low-rent upstairs quadplex apartment, a gracious offer of the owners, Tom Duke and David Cadden, two close friends in my church. They waived the deposit and reduced the first month's rent by half to get me started because I was newly hired after being unemployed for one of the first times in my life and had very little cash on hand. My downstairs neighbors smoked and it daily came through the floors or vents and I asked them repeatedly to stop. The apartment agreement prohibited smoking, but they continued to smoke indoors for the year and a half I lived there.

A coworker named Leah offered me her brother-in-law's house to rent, but the rent was $100 more and I was afraid that may be too much. About a year later my house sold, and I made an offer on a home. Mine was the winning bid and the sellers stated all heat and air conditioning was in working condition. The loan was approved, and the inspection revealed that neither the heat nor the air conditioning was working. In fact, they both were completely rotted out. Both had to be replaced, and the price was more than I could afford and I had already given up the apartment to a friend, who had already terminated his former lease. I was two weeks from being without a place to stay.

I went to work the next day and laughingly announced I would be homeless in two weeks. My friend Leah said, "Well, I think my brother-in-law's tenant is leaving this week, and he may need a new tenant." I called and he did. Once again, no deposit and no lease. I could leave anytime. It was done! I was heading to 2141 Balfour Street, Augusta, Georgia...

By this time two things had happened. My son and daughter had become Christians, and God changed them in so many ways I cannot count. My son married a wonderful woman named Taylor and they began a new life with each other and Christ. In four years' time, I had four grandsons, Preston, Bentley, Tatum, and Cadden, the best a grandfather could ask for. My daughter, Sierra was next to decide to follow Christ. She was now a freshman in college, and we had a very broken relationship. She hated me as she should have because of my anger issues and being unplugged from being the father that I used to dream about but never became. She had a friend named Logan that shared with her how to become a Christian and she fully gave her life to the Lord. A short time later she called me on the phone and said

"Dad, I am a Christian. I prayed to receive Christ as my personal savior," and then screamed, "Dad, I love you!"

My son now leads worship at our church, and he has grown out of being addicted to drugs and into a sincere believer in Christ and a growing relationship with the Lord and his family. Sierra was planning on going on staff with Campus Outreach and had, as her college pastor told me, discipled countless numbers of girls, including his daughter. Those plans changed when the Lord brought Drew Patrick into her life. Now she has finished college, married and is at seminary with Drew, who is studying to be a pastor.

Top row Tyler & Taylor Padgett bottom row left to right Grandson's Preston, Bentley, Cadden, and Tatum

As I walked down the aisle with my daughter to give her hand to a grown man weeping for joy over his new bride, I could barely believe how much life had changed. He was God's gift to my daughter as was she to him. It was all so unrecognizably good. It could have turned out so differently but by God's grace alone it didn't. You can't make this stuff up!

My youngest daughter, Ellie, has been God's gift to me. We started reading our bible together every night before bed and praying before we go to sleep. We have had a weeklong mission trip together to Jamaica, so many other adventures, and we are so much alike. She wants six kids, so I have been praying for her husband for almost nine years now. I say this laughing out loud!

I tell Ellie that my desire for her is that she would not have to go through the destruction and heartbreak that Tyler, Sierra and I went through in order to get it right with the Lord. It does not have to be that way.   So I am leaving a blank space here _____

_____

_____ ... and I will come back years from now and let you know how it turned out for Ellie.

My son in law Drew Patrick and daughter Sierra

Daughters Ellie & Sierra

Drew and Sierra holding up Sonogram of their soon to be born son Everett Wayne Patrick! My GRANDSON! :)

Ellie Padgett

Drew & Sierra and newest grandson Everett Wayne Patrick born
Nov. 4, 2021

His Full Name Is Adalbert Leslie Glaicz (Albert)

So, I pack up my stuff and I move to 2141 Balfour Street, Augusta, Georgia. As I arrive, I meet the outgoing tenant, George. We talk for quite some time and he warns me about the next door neighbor at 2139 Balfour Street. He calls him the old man and describes him with the worst of descriptions. He tells me of taking him to the drug store and having to physically remove him from the store because he was racially insulting others in the store. George said I told him, "I will never help you again, old man." He said no one likes him, and he is hateful, and he's just a bad person. I hoped that this was not turning out to be a very bad decision and that maybe it was just a clash of two stubborn people.

So I move into the rental house and I was so thankful that I would have a back yard for Ellie and my grandsons to play in. It was the perfect size at about 1300 square feet with 3 bedrooms, enough to have my grandsons sleep over. My job was going well so I felt that I could handle the rent, plus I had savings since the other house sold.

While outside cutting my grass, my next door neighbor walks over to the fence and introduces himself to me. He said, hi, my name is Albert Glaicz." He speaks to me with a rich French accent and is wearing a flat cap. He looks to me to be about 5 foot 3 inches tall, and I later I find out his full name is Adalbert Leslie Glaicz. He was sturdily built and had a very firm handshake. His hair was white, and he wore a goatee. We discussed the weather and other insignificant

33

things and I found him to be intelligent, engaging, and nothing like how George had described him. He tells me he is ninety years old, and I am stunned to hear that. He looks to be around seventy, and his mind was very sharp. We briefly discuss the war since he and my father fought in it. Albert says to me that he served in the Canadian army. . I remember the Canadians fared poorly on D-Day, so I ask him about that. His answer was vague, and he would not continue that conversation. I thought it was a strange reaction and decide not to ask any more questions. Later I find out that he grew up in France and was in the French military, then moved to Canada after the war.

I share with him stories of my divorce so he will understand why I am moving in, and he shares about his divorce. He made a quick comment as to how bad his ex-wife was but nothing more negative that afternoon.

Fence Talks

About a week or so had gone by and he came over to the fence and began telling a dirty joke. I did not laugh, so he tried another one only to get the same response. I shared with him that I am a Christian, and that was the reason I didn't want to hear those kinds of jokes. He looked a little surprised but didn't let that get in the way of his next joke. He just cleaned it up so we could both laugh together. What was most funny is that he would tell me a joke, and I would not understand half of what he said, partly because of my poor hearing and partly because of his heavy French accent. But as time passed, I begin to learn how to understand his broken French/English and we could carry on good conversations.

I work at the local cable company and he knew that, so on his visit to pay his bill (he drove to each location to pay all his bills) he mentioned I was his neighbor. Soon the ladies up front told me that on each visit he would tell them jokes. Most were off color, and they were always amazed at his energy and his dislike of his ex-wives. They often said, "He is a handful."

Albert and I continued to have many fence talks, and he seemed more and more willing to become open about his life. He told me that he was an orphan that he was left as an infant on the Catholic orphanage steps by his mother. He lived in the orphanage until the war. He had very sad stories of not enough food and living with constant hunger. He said he never experienced being loved except for one nun who was different. "She really cared," is how he put it. Later he brought up his ex-wife and mentioned her unfaithfulness. With this story his emotions rose to a new level, not extreme but certainly elevated more than I had seen before. This is where the mask first slipped down his face, and I saw for the first time who he may be, but it was nothing that made me feel uncomfortable or that seemed unusual.

Albert and I had many conversations as time passed, and I now felt comfortable inviting him to my church because of his comfort level with me. He accepted, and I picked him up the following Sunday. He comes out of his house dressed very dapper, with his wool flat cap and sport coat. My church is a very relaxed, come-as-you-are congregation so there were no issues one way or the other regarding how he dressed. On the way to church he made it clear to me he wanted me to not mention his age, especially to the ladies. I laughed inside that at ninety years old, he is still looking for companionship, and so I honored his wish. When we arrive, I begin introducing him to others and with each introduction, if the person engaged in any conversation with him, he brought up one particular story. He would start off by saying "Did you know the United States mistreated the veterans early in their history and turned on them with violence in Washington?" He repeated this too many of the men and it seemed an odd thing to me but later as I thought about it, I could only guess that it was to show them how well read he was.

He decided to come back to church with me the next week but let it be known to Pastor Rod that his sermon was too long. On the way home from church He begins to tell me about other churches he had attended and with each story he reveals that he had a falling out with the pastors at all of them. I suspected that it would not be long before Pastor Rod would be next, and I was right.

Albert is an artist and has painted 40 or more paintings. He decided he would like to give one or two to the church, but he had already decided where the paintings would be placed. It was going to be on his terms. Pastor Rod never agreed to the terms for many reasons, one being he was not sure what the picture may contain and two he always thinks and prays through something if he is unsure... Pastor Rod's need to think through it made Albert mad, and he stopped coming with me from that point on. I was a bit surprised at how quick he was to cancel his interest in coming to church even though he had not been told no to the idea of where he wants the picture to hang. He had no interest in discussing the matter with our Pastor, it was simply over for him to ever attend church here again. I was glad that he did not cancel our new friendship though. We continued with our fence talks and everything else seem to stay normal. It did cross my mind though as I thought about the bigger picture of what I was noticing. First, I wondered, does this explain why in almost a year of me living next to him I have not seen a friend or family member come visit him. Secondly, it seems strange that he appears to want friends in his life, yet he is so at ease to say good riddance to anyone who does not do exactly as he wishes. It will not be too much longer before both questions will soon be answered.

37

Tighty Whittie

Albert was very funny sometimes, even when he didn't mean to be, and he could have a very good sense of humor. He was unpredictable to say the least and at times could just leave me speechless. He was so colorful of a personality. One Saturday he came over to my house and rang the doorbell. His normal doorbell ring was to press it over and over again repeatedly, so when I finally got to the door I was almost mad. I invited him in and noticed he was moving slowly and holding his shoulder. I asked, "Albert, what happened to you? Are you hurt?"

He said, "I was on top of my house doing a repair, and I slipped and fell off the roof."

I asked, "What in the world were you doing on your roof?"

He said "I was putting tar around my chimney." I told him he should never do that again, that could have killed him, to which he said, "That's the third time I have fallen off my roof, and here is how you do it without getting hurt." He explained to me, "as my feet slip out from under me and I begin rolling down the roof, just when I am about to go over the edge, I relax. If you relax you won't break anything." My mouth stood open in astonishment and I couldn't help but laugh out loud. Albert began laughing with me.

I said, "So you are a professional roof faller?" We laughed again.

Another time I was outside by the fence where we always met, and it was dusk outside. I was finishing some yard work and I noticed Albert coming toward the fence. Something seemed strange but I couldn't figure out what. As he continued to get closer I realized he was in nothing but his white tank top tee shirt and his Tighty Whittie underwear. He wanted to carry on a conversation standing there in his underwear. I was trying not to laugh at the absurdity that he has walked out into the yard dressed like this and we have neighbors on 3 different sides with a clear view of us standing there talking. I am wondering how I will explain to our neighbors why two grown men would be conversing over the fence as usual, except the one in his nineties was wearing only underwear! All I could think about was I must come up with a quick reason that I need to go inside my house...NOW! I have no idea to this day what the reason I gave him was but whatever I said worked and I walked as quick as I could to my back door.

To this very day I still think Albert did that just to mess with me, but I will never know for sure.

"That's for you, it's not for me!"

Albert had other peculiarities. He wore this one baseball type cap the most, and it was filthy. I think this was his everyday work hat. I had seen it almost every time he would be outside, but I had never noticed what was written on the front. It said Joshua 24:15, a life verse of mine. I was surprised, and asked where he got it. He said he wasn't sure. I asked if he knew what that verse says, and he said no.

I said, "Albert, that is one of my favorite verses and it says 'and if it seems evil to you to serve the Lord, choose for yourselves this day whom you will serve. As for me and my house, we will serve the Lord.' Albert," I continued, "I made a decision about four and a half years ago that I was going to serve the Lord." I explained my past to him and how God rescued me once again and that I wanted to live my life following Christ till the day I die." He didn't react much to that, making only the slight remark, "That's for you, not for me."

As we continued having more conversations about many things, his anger, hatred, and utter contempt for almost everyone began to show more and more.

In the movie *The Fellowship of the Ring*, Bilbo Baggins's face changed into a scary possessed-looking face because he wanted to keep the ring so bad. That sort of describes how Albert face would look as he was telling his stories of how so many have done him wrong. He often talked about his ex-wives and especially one that he said cheated on him. I asked him one day, "what causes you to go

40

back and repeat all those stories of how much you hate and despise your ex-wives?" He said, "I wake up in the morning, and I have a thought about something they did to me, and then I think of other things and begin to feel the anger. And as more of the day passes my anger gets worse. This happens every day, over and over." I said "Albert, have you ever heard me mention my two ex-wives in anger or mention anything they did to me?" A little shocked, he said, "No,." I said to him, "the reason why is because I have done so many wrong things in my life that I have needed forgiveness for, so how can I now not forgive them of anything they did to me? I explained, "When you wake up and begin carrying those hot coals of anger and unforgiveness around in your hands looking to throw them on these wives, all the while you are burning your own hands as you grasp them near you." I said, "Albert, only God can give you the ability to forgive them, but first you need forgiveness of your own sins." I shared Romans 3:23, "For we all have sinned and fall short of the glory of God," and that Romans 6:23 says "Our wages of sin is death, but the gift of God is eternal life in Christ Jesus our Lord." I recited John 1:12, "but to all who did receive Him, to them who believed in His name, He gave the right to become children of God, "Albert, God can forgive all your sins and give you the power to forgive everyone who has hurt you. You are a very hurt man, Albert, would you like to have God remove all this hurt and give you a brand new heart?" He said, "That's for you, it's not for me!"

Albert Was the Main Reason

By this time, I had made two other offers to buy a home. Both times I was uneasy in my heart about leaving here because of Albert, but it seemed sensible to not throw rental money away. On the first home I offered less than the owner was asking and he accepted a better offer. With the second house, my friend Sharon the real estate agent told me to offer more than the owner was asking, which I did, but another offer was higher.

I gave it sometime between the last 2 offers and asked to see this little dream house that was priced right. I make an offer and Sharon calls back and says, "it's under contract." I found another house in the country and made an offer, but I was outbid again, even though I offered a lot more than they asked. After losing out one more home I said that's enough. I told Sharon after six tries I am tired. I think I need to stay here at 2141 Balfour St. I felt there was a reason God wanted me here and Albert was the main reason, but I also felt that it was foolish to pay rent and not purchase a home. I even had a prayer that I said to God several times in which I would do the math for God on how much I was throwing away on rent. It went something like this. I would say to God, "I am paying $650 rent per month and at the end of 1 year I have thrown away $7800 on rent. I am in my second year now and at the end of 2 years I will have wasted $15,600. Please open me up a door of some place that I can begin to pay down a mortgage on a home as quickly as I can. As I would do often when I pray, I would be silent and just listen to see if I was given any impression in my mind and heart of God speaking to me. I want to be careful here and tell you the reader that I have never heard God speak to me verbally. I have never seen God, and I have never been visited by any angels. The primary way that I hear God is that there will be a scripture that will come to my mind that will apply to the situation I am in. In this situation, each time I would pray I would repeatedly recall this verse of scripture in my mind, Matthew 6:33 "But seek first the Kingdom of God and His righteousness, and all these things will be added to you" I believed that this was my answer from God, but I didn't like the answer. I just wanted to have my answer now and this seemed like I was just hearing "Later".

Months later in the winter at our daughters' volleyball game, Sharon mentions this cute house somewhere, I said I want to see it. When she walks away, my heart begins racing, and I have a fear come over me that I can't explain. I get up, hunt her down and say, almost fearfully, "I don't want to see it." I feel I need to stay where I am. She seemed a little startled by my urgency. I tell her, I'm sorry I just really feel I do need to stay at my current location." I would never again ask her about any other homes while Albert was still living.

Not Real Heart Questions

One afternoon Albert said, "I need to talk to you about something."

The tone of his voice was so serious I became curious and said "Go ahead. What's on your mind?" He states that he would like me to be the Executor of his Will after his death. He said, I will give you a certain amount of money if you will do this. He said on top of what I give you, I want you to give an additional amount of money that I have to the Indian Children's Home and to St. Jude's Children Hospital. I could tell by what he wanted to give to, that children were dear to his heart. I remembered him telling me several times he had a camper and he gave it to the McCormick South Carolina Children's Home but, later had a falling out with them because he didn't get the recognition, he felt he should have.

I told him I would not be able to give him an answer until I prayed about it and sought council from my pastor. Before I was able to talk to Pastor Rod, I felt a strong hesitation in my heart to not do it. I sensed from the Lord that if I accepted the money it would change everything, and my pastor said the same thing when we talked. I felt like if I accepted the money and responsibility that he would never know if I was doing something for him because of money or because I loved and cared about him. The words came to my mind that I would tell him. So I talked with Albert a few days later and said, "Albert, I cannot accept your offer because of this reason, it's not that I couldn't use any money, but I don't want your money. I want your soul, and I want to spend an eternity with you in heaven." To my surprise, He wasn't upset with me at all and he even was encouraging me to purchase the house I was renting. Even though I considered it, I never felt like that was the thing I wanted to do. I could then tell through this exchange that he trusted me and we were making some progress in our relationship.

Albert began to ask me a lot of questions about God in the coming months. Most of the questions were "gotcha questions and not real heart questions like" "If there is a God, why is there so much evil in the world?" "What about all the people in the world who have other gods, what's going to happen to them?" He mentioned the death, starvation, and evil of the war and said, "If there was a god, why did he not stop that?" I really thought sometimes about asking him this question just to see what he might say but I didn't want him to think I was being insensitive to his questions. I wanted to ask him this question, "Albert if I could answer all of these questions perfectly and not get anything wrong and you perfectly understood the answer, would you then be ready and willing to give the Lord your heart and follow Him?

I gave him the best answers that I could, but inwardly I felt his questions were only mental jousting and not real heart questions.

Painful To Hear His Venom

Albert did seem to want to talk more and more and even invited me to dinner one night. I accepted and really looked forward to it because he was an Executive Chef by profession and said he worked at the Canadian Embassy and once fed 3,000 people. He named many exclusive hotels in California where he was the Executive Chef and talked about a lot of dishes he served that were his specialty. He told stories of choosing the menus and cooking for very important people. This particular night he made spaghetti, and it was delicious. It certainly had the taste unique to homemade. He showed me paintings he had done and discussed places he had traveled to all over the world, but, like many times before, the discussion eventually changed to his ex-wives and his hatred for them. He mentioned kids that they birth but they were not his own. For hours that night Albert went from subject to subject and all were about his hatred for each person or persons. He described his vile neighbors that had poisoned his trees and other neighbors that were "garbage," his favorite word for people. It was painful to hear his venom for everyone.

For the first time the mask he wore was completely off now. I have never before seen someone so consumed by hatred and distrust. It was a long night of story after story of him cursing everyone who had betrayed him. By the end of our night talking I said to him again, "Albert, God can give you forgiveness for all those who have hurt you. You are one of the most hurt men I have ever known, but He can take that away."

Then in what would become his most common answer he says, waiving his hand downward, "that's for you, but not for me." I went home that night especially troubled. I prayed for him as he had become a part of my prayers most days.

Randy and Rod Never Gave Up!

Something in me said, "Don't give up on Albert." I have been taught by example by two people, Randy Weeaks and Rod Addison the Importance of never giving up and it was my turn to apply these valuable lessons with others. Below you will read two stories of Randy Weeaks and Rod Addison on how to not give up.

When I was in my last year of seminary, I got a new roommate. His name was Randy Weeaks. He was a hulking offensive lineman who played college football for East Central Oklahoma University. Randy and I quickly became great friends.

I had a painting business to help work my way through seminary, and he started working for me, which meant we shared lots of time together painting and as roommates. He was as real as it gets, and I loved him for that. After seminary he started a church in Texas and it soon became one of the fastest growing churches in America. While he was doing this, I was spiraling downward out of control toward what would become almost a thirty-year path of being out of fellowship with Christ. The most remarkable thing about Randy is that he never gave up on me. Randy would contact me by phone at the very least every 6 months and check on me. Sometimes he would call, and I would be drunk, and he would know it, but he still let me know he loved me and by his action alone he would not give up on me.

I know Randy had one thousand things to do as pastor, but he would take his time out for me. He would not give up. After I made the decision to return to Christ, the calls became much more frequent as he helped me get my legs back underneath me and get stronger so I could once again stand. It's been ten years since then, and Randy still calls regularly. That is almost forty years in all now that he has invested in me. He would not give up!

The second person is my pastor, Rod Addison. My family began attending West Town Community Church because our neighbors Greg and Kendall Porter invited us to come. It would become the place of hope for me, a place where I could heal, grow, and once again become a fully devoted follower of Jesus Christ. But before any of that could happen, I had to come to the end of myself.

Rod did this sort of spiritual dance with me that would continue for about two years before I came to my senses. As I needed him, he would be there, and when I pushed away, he would not pressure me. I believe if he had pressured me, I would have just stopped coming. Each time I would reach out to him thinking I might be ready to let go of my addictions, he was there, and he would give me great wisdom and help. But that wisdom required my choice to leave where I was and once again follow Christ. My greatest fear was that if I made the choice to follow Christ, I did not want to fall again and hurt more people as I had done in the past. Eventually I came to the end of all my running and even this fear could no longer hold me back. Rod never gave up on me. To this very day, he and I have met together hundreds of times. Many of those times I would tell him, "I feel like I am losing my balance." He would give great instruction and counsel. He knows my failures, but he would not give up on me! Randy and Rod never gave up!

My greatest desire now was to see Albert rescued from all of his hurts, habits and hang ups, and see what God could do when He changes the heart of a man in his 90's. I did not want to give up on Albert! (Most of the time) ☺

From right to left, Daughter Skyler, Wife Vangie, Pastor Rod, Son Hunter, Grandchildren Sam and Emma Leigh Martin.

This Was In No Way a Shock to God

Cadden Padgett　　　*Cadden Padgett*　　　*Cadden Padgett*

One afternoon Albert asked me what happened to my youngest grandson's hands. My grandson Cadden was born with no hands and just one finger, and Albert was drawn to him and seemed to have compassion for him. He even gave him one of his paintings. I told him that neither side of Tyler's family or Taylor's family had ever had a birth defect until Cadden. He was silent and had no response. My son Tyler and his wife Taylor announced that they were going to have another child, and this would be my fourth grandson. If the baby was a boy, they would name him Cadden after David and Marie Cadden, our close friends. The Cadden's had given Tyler and Taylor a minivan when they were just starting out in their marriage because the Pontiac Grand Am two-door car was not going to work for all of them. Tyler and Taylor cried tears of joy on this Christmas Eve gift, and this van became a huge blessing as Taylor developed her catering business and later become a professional wedding planner.

One afternoon Taylor had called me at work, but I missed the call. She was at the doctor's office having a sonogram. Our understanding of God was about to be enlarged and magnified, and the baby boy in the sonogram image would be used to change people's lives and glorify our Heavenly Father even before he ever arrived. What my son and daughter-in-law and literally our entire combined families were about to see would change and reshape us all. But it would be painful for us before it became beautiful. And because I missed Taylor's phone call, I received this text:

> Given the news that our little baby boy had Ectrodactyly (or ECC). By the looks of the sonogram his forearms are about half the length that they should be. He has very short thumbs and he's missing one finger on each hand. He also only has one bone in each arm where we normally have two. We are praising God that it's not a mental condition like the doctors originally suspected. He will be able to do everything that a normal person can do, he will just look a little different.

As I was reading those words it was like glass dishes were perpetually falling out of the cabinet, shattering onto a concrete floor. I felt helpless as splintered, fragile thoughts tumbled clumsily from my mind: how will he be able to handle all the things he will need to do? How will this effect Taylor and Tyler because they already have three sons, and they are all young and now this? How will Cadden be treated all his life? And then I read these words in the text:

> Though it was a big shock to us, this was in no way a shock to God. He has a purpose for our sweet boy. "For you created my inmost being; you knit me together in my mother's womb. I praise you because I am fearfully and wonderfully made; your works are wonderful, I know that full well. My frame was not hidden from you when I was made in the secret place, when I was woven together in the depths of the earth. Your eyes saw my unformed body; all the days ordained for me were written in your book before one of them came to be." (Psalm 139:13-15)

And suddenly the crashing in my mind and heart stopped, and joy flooded my soul. Hope burst in my heart, fear left me and certainty that Cadden was God's gift who will bring glory to God in ways I could not imagine took its place. I walked outside work with tears of joy running down my face. I fell on my knees right in front of my office at the first column. I praised God and thanked Him for who Cadden is and who he will be in the hands of our faithful heavenly father. Taylor seemed to me to be shocked but had a calm resolve that was beyond explanation. Her faith defied her young age. I give credit to her dad and mom, Wayne and Tracie Anderson, for being the example all their lives of people who have walked by faith with God.

It would be a few more days before my son Tyler would have his "aha" moment, but God had already laid His plan in place with perfect, impeccable timing. Tyler drove to see his mother in Spartanburg, South Carolina they were meeting at a restaurant to discuss what had transpired. Pastor Rod had called my son and was talking to him as he arrived at the restaurant, but Tyler's heart was so troubled that as Tyler described it, "It was like Pastor Rod was saying Blah, Blah, Blah." That's no reflection on Pastor Rod. He wears the heavyweight championship belt as "The Greatest Pastor," but God had another means of speaking to Tyler this time.

When they hung up the phone, Tyler recognized a couple walking towards the restaurant. They stopped, and as they were talking, Tyler shared the news with them about Cadden, remembering that their daughter was born without a leg. They shared with him that her being born that way was the most life-changing experience for them in their family and relationship with God. They encouraged him and told him to trust that God would use this boy in a magnificent way. They asked if they could pray for him, and he said yes. They circled him and put their arms on his shoulders and prayed as Tyler cried. All of this took place in front of the window where Tyler's mom sat with her sister. When Tyler walked in his mom said "Tyler, when I saw you out there with them, knowing their story, I said to Lori, 'Lori, there is a God in heaven.'"

God would use that experience in his mom's life to change her and after that day Tyler has had so much peace. God has used Cadden to change Tyler, and Tyler has never been the same. God used Cadden in Albert's life also. Ultimately God's plan is to rescue us all from our sins and then to use us as His shining examples of how His grace can transform us into new people, quite unlike who we were before and give those who do not know Him hope. Before he was born, Cadden already had a history of God using him. His life is and will continue to be a life of exciting adventures of radiating God's glory.

Top row David, wife Marie, son DJ, bottom row left to right daughters Caroline & Madeline.

His First Real Heart Questions

Albert's adventure with Cadden began with the incessant ringing of my doorbell one afternoon. When I answered, There stood Albert, out of breath and angry. I was a little shocked as I had never seen him like this before. I said, "Albert, come in, and what's the matter?" He sat down and motioned for me to be patient. I said, "Take your time, Albert, are you alright? Do you need water?" He shook his head no, he then raised his finger to emphasize his point, and said, "If God is such a good God, why would He do that to your grandson?" I could immediately tell that this thought had been on his mind in a profound way for some time. It was the first time that he asked me a question that was not a "Gotcha Question". It seemed to me that this question came from the depth of his soul and he was crying out inside. He seemed to be saying why has God treated me like this and now He is doing the same to your grandson. I felt in my heart that this question had a lot to do with his own pain of being an orphan and having experienced so little love. I think it was the same question he had as to why his wives did not love him, and why according to his thinking, did they betray him. So, I begin to try and answer him the best I can.

I asked if he was talking about Cadden. He shook his head yes. Anger was written all over his face. Knowing him he had been thinking about this for most of the day and his anger had boiled over, and he just poured it out all over me. I inwardly asked God quickly, "Please, help me speak as you would speak."

The first thought that came to my mind was not original to me. I think I saw this in the movie *God's Not Dead*, and it seemed to be the best answer. So I said "Albert, first of all, I want to tell you I am a little taken aback by your question, and the reason is I don't understand how you can be mad at a God you do not believe in, it's akin to hating Santa Claus, even though I know he is a fictional character." Then I said, "The Bible says in Roman 1:20, *'for since the creation of the world His (meaning God) invisible qualities, His eternal power and divine nature, have been clearly seen, being understood from His workmanship, so that men are without excuse.* Albert, what you have really just told me is that you do indeed believe in God and you are very mad at Him."

"Secondly, I want to ask you this? What if God could take Cadden and uses him in a way that if one person gave their life to Christ and lived for an eternity with Christ, wouldn't that be an amazing thing? I see one day in my imagination that maybe Cadden speaks to a large group of people and raises his one and only finger toward heaven and says the words 'there is only one way to God and that is through His Son who died on the cross for your sins' and pointing his one finger at them he asks, 'would you be willing to give Him your life and follow Him?'"

Albert did not answer but seemed to just be in deep thought, so I continued. "Do you want to ask Christ to be your Savior and take away all your pain, hatred, and loneliness and give you back hope?'"

He simply said, "No." and after some small talk, he shuffled his way home.

After some thinking back on this day, I came to a conclusion God did indeed use Cadden that day. Albert would have never come over and asked what I believe were his first real heart questions, but I also believe his rejection of Christ that day started a greater struggle within him because he became very hostile toward me in a way he had never done before.

I Was Enabling Him

In the coming days and months Albert grew more and more agitated, not only with me, but also with the trash collectors, the mailman, and neighbors. It seemed as though he was taking offense against everyone. When I would be outside he would hunt me down to tell me that day's conflicts he had with people. It was like a dump truck backing up to me and unloading its full contents of stinking garbage on top of me. He would be cursing each person and using his favorite phrase and say each person was "A piece of garbage. "I prayed for God to give me wisdom as how to handle it. It was such a major change in him. He was anger filled and despised everyone. At the same time this was going on new battle began in my own heart. I started having the thoughts that I had to make a change in how I was handling this, and I began to wrestle with the idea that I had to make a change in what we talked about. The impression I got in my heart was that I was enabling him. Sort of like what a spouse might do to an alcoholic husband or wife. The enabler will just choose to ignore the problem just keep the peace, but all that really does is allow the issue to destroy the alcoholic person little by little. My thoughts were like this, by giving him my ears to listen to this hatred and not stopping it, all I was doing was encouraging him to continue. I was very concerned about how I should talk to him because I did not want to risk our relationship, yet I felt we had fallen into a rut of him just spewing his cruel hatred out about everyone and me listening. I decided to seek counsel from my pastor and he agreed that I should take some new steps to see if I could change the conversation. I felt it was the right thing to do to have a talk with Albert but I also dreaded it because I believed this could be the conversation that ends our friendship at least on his part. One afternoon I felt I could not delay in talking to him any longer so I prayed that God would help me say the right words before I began to walk to his house. I was relatively sure this might not go so well, but the alternative of not dealing with it seemed worse. I sincerely did not want to destroy any future opportunities of being a friend and witness for Christ in his life but I was convinced that this had to be done. I loved this crusty, bitter, and hurt man, and it pained me taking each step toward his door. I rang his doorbell and when he answered the door, I asked if I could come in and talk, and he said yes. We sat down at his dining room table, which was stacked high with bills, magazines, glasses, and other items.. I started by saying, "Albert, I care about you. I want so much for you to be set free of the hatred you have for so many people, but I have to tell you that we must have a change in our conversations. I cannot give you my ears to listen to your hate-filled words toward your ex-wives, neighbors, and all others. I want to be your friend and a good neighbor, but we cannot continue with these types of conversations. We have other things we can talk about, and I hope we will, but if this cannot stop, then I cannot listen to it anymore. I am guilty of enabling you by giving you my ears to hear this." Is this something you are willing for us to change so we can continue our friendship?

He looked at me and, without hesitation, said "There's the door. You can leave now."

I stood up and said, "I am sorry we can't work through this, and I want you to know I love you and God loves you. If you need me for anything, I am here."

As I walked back to my house, I felt as defeated as I have ever felt. It seemed impossible that he and I would ever talk again. I wondered then if he would die without knowing Christ as His savior. But even with the overwhelming thoughts about this, I had a peace come over me that I can't explain. I said to God, "I love Albert but he is loved by you far more than I could love him, so I ask that you to contend for his heart. Please, Lord, don't let him die without knowing you. I surrender him to You, Lord. Your will be done in his life." The following months were strange and very difficult. I would see Albert in his yard looking so alone, and I would pray for him. I prayed for him almost daily. It wasn't like I had to plan it or write it down to remember. He would just come to my thoughts, and I would pray. When I walked outside and Albert would see me, he would wait till he knew I looked his way and then he would wave his hand downward and I could imagine hearing him say to himself, "You piece of garbage, I will have nothing to do with you!" Then he would turn his back on me and not look again. This was repeated day after day. A few weeks later I noticed Albert had a visitor in his backyard one day and it looked like he was selling something of his to the person. I had to clean my yard up, so I went outside to pick up stuff and as I did, he looked at me and nudged the guy he was talking to and wanted him to look over at me. When the guy looked at me, I could hear Albert speaking but could not understand what he said because we were too far apart. Then he waived his hand downward and shook his head in discuss at me then looked the other way. In my imagination I could hear him say the words to the man "He is a piece of garbage." I was sure now that I was on his ever-expanding list of people who are garbage. This hurt my heart deeply not because I had become dependent on our friendship but because I felt as though I may never be let back into his life again and this is how things would just end. My hope for him knowing the Lord was growing small but I continued to pray even more for him as time moved on.

This Hurt My Heart Deeply

When I moved into my rental home next door to Albert, I noticed that Albert's fence consisted of a chain link fence in the front yard. He said he did that to keep the leaves of the trees from my house and others from coming into his yard. It seemed to make sense to me, but what didn't make sense is he also had three more layers of fence with three different kinds of wire that were applied to this fence. That was strange and, although I never asked why, I was soon to find out. There was a span of about four feet from the end of this fence in the front yard to a very large pine tree almost at the road we lived on. He began construction on a new fence at this spot even though there had never been any leaves blown into his yard since I had moved in. It consisted of part plastic and part metal pieces he had laying around, and he used a lot of tie wire to close this off. To say it was ugly would be a compliment. I really believe he had developed a way of telling his neighbor through building another layer of fence that he was done with them. It seemed like it was a message to me. After several months, the plastic became brittle, and a strong storm broke it down. Albert came over to my house and rang the doorbell (at least 20 times back to back like a machine gun) and in a state of fury he first blamed me and then my ex-wife, saying she backed into it. Both were dead wrong, but he was in a rage when telling me this. I asked, "Albert, do you think I am so petty that I would do something like that?" He gave me the downward hand wave and began to shuffle his way back to his house. It was crazy as well as sad. It appears he fed off conflict and I was his newest target.

In the next few months I had the impression in my heart to fight fire with kindness. I know that's not like me by nature, so I was reasonably sure this was something the Lord was asking me to do. So in the coming months I took him certain things to eat that I thought he may not be able to resist, like cold watermelon (he took it), homemade peach ice cream (he took it, but not before telling me the texture was not right), and barbecue chicken (he snarled at it and said nothing but took it and shut the front door with the chicken still in his hand). For some reason none of these responses bothered me and so I continued doing it from time to time.

A short time later Albert began work on a much better fence with very durable materials that he had bought recently. He had new metal reinforcement and all new stakes, I believe he was reiterating his sentiment and by doing this saying to me, "I still hate you."

Newly constructed fence just for me

Layers of fence constructed for past renters

Biggest Conflict We Ever Had

One afternoon on a Saturday Albert came over to my house in what would be the biggest conflict we ever had. After his ringing the doorbell repeatedly just to get the conflict going, he started the conversation like this. "I want you to move your stuff and give me access to my wood fence." He was referencing a section at the other end of the front lawn fence. He said "I want to paint it, and by law you have to give me this room."

I was having a hard time understanding him because he was so worked up with anger and he was breathing with short breaths. I wanted to know exactly what he wanted me to do, so I repeated what I thought he said by saying, "Albert, are you asking me to move my car, or is there something else you need me to do"?

He roared back at me in an angry voice I had never heard him use and pointed his finger at me and said as he cursed at me, "I am not asking you to do anything, I am telling you that you will move your stuff."

At this point I was angry and I said to him, "Let me be clear about something. My youngest daughter Ellie can hear this and is listening in the other room, so I want you to know you can come over here and ask me to do anything for you, and I will do it if at all possible. In fact, I will do this job for you, but what you will not do, is come into my house and demand of me that I do this." Furthermore you cannot come into my house and use the language you have used either."

He immediately walked out without a word. I later saw him sitting on his front steps catching his breath. That afternoon I walked outside to talk to him because he was in the back yard. I asked him to come to the fence. He refused, and I insisted, saying, "Please. Come over here"

He came, and I apologized for my anger but still said to him, "Albert, you are a grown man, just like me. If I wanted you to do something for me I would ask you politely, but I would never come to you and tell you 'you will do this for me.' You would just tell me to kiss your butt and walk away if I did. So going forward, if there is anything you need, ask me, and I will be glad to help."

To my amazement he started talking to me about other stuff after this talk, and later brought up his ex-wives again. I said to him, "Albert, hating on these other women is eating your soul up. How long has it been since you have seen them?" He said fifteen years. I said, "For fifteen years you have been wishing that they would die?"

He stopped me and raised that one finger and said, "I never said I want them to die. I want them to live and the maggots eat them, but they can't die."

I said, "Only God can help you, Albert!" At that, I went inside and talked to my daughter Ellie, and we prayed together, as we had many times, for him.

Face Down In the Grass

In the coming months I would see him outside working on things, and one time he had an open book sitting in the entrance of his workshop. I wondered if it was the bible so I went outside and we talked briefly. I asked him what he was reading. He told me, but it was not the bible. I asked him had he ever read the bible, and he answered, "No." It became apparent to me that he had adopted other people's arguments against God and the bible but had never personally read it. I made the suggestion to him to start reading it, beginning with the book of Matthew. He gave me no indication that he would take me up on that.

In the following weeks I did not see him at all. When that happened in the past I would go over and check on him, so I did just that. I rang his doorbell, and after a while he answered the door in his underwear, even though it was the middle of the day. He seemed frail. I told him I had not seen him in the yard, so I was there to check on him. He explained that he had a heart attack in his front yard that the neighbors had seen him face down in the grass and had called the ambulance. I asked him how he was he doing, and he answered, "I am tired. All I want to do is sleep."

I asked him if I could get anything for him, and he said no. There still was a coldness between us relationally, and he was not willing to let it go. I told him if he needed me for anything, to call me. I gave him my number and told him to take care. I went home now with a new sense of urgency in my heart. I cried out to God for this man. I had no idea how long he had left, but it didn't look good to me. He still had his mind, but his body was weak. I couldn't imagine going through so much with Albert only to lose him for an eternity because he would not come to the end of himself and let Christ save him.

One day I came home to Albert standing on the front steps of his house, so I walked over to check on him. I asked him if he was ok, and he said no. I asked what was wrong, and he put his hand on his chest and said it was his heart. He said, "I am having a heart attack right now." Alarmed I said him, "Let me call an ambulance!" but he said "No, a lady name Rochelle is coming to pick me up right now and take me to the hospital." She pulled in almost immediately and I helped Albert into the car, and she admitted him to the hospital and then called me to let me know he was okay.

I went to see him, but no one by that name was listed as a patient. I later went to his mailbox and discovered how he spells his last name, then called and talked to him. He said they wanted to do surgery but he was not going to allow that, and he wanted to go home for good. He said, "No more trips to the hospital."

Heap Burning Coals on His Head

That weekend I was cutting my grass, and as I was finishing on that hot Georgia summer day, I noticed Albert's grass needed cutting. The next thought I had was I need to go cut his grass. I was unsure if this was my thinking or was God asking me to do this. I started a conversation with the Lord in my mind that went like this. "If I go over there and cut his grass, he will come out angry and run me off his property or worse call the police and tell them to hand cuff me for trespassing because officially the war he was having with me wasn't over, and he had never said there was a truce.

Then I backed that up with my own problems of just being lazy and said, "I am too tired, hot, and thirsty to cut his grass." Then the thought came to my mind, *"If your enemy is hungry, give him food to eat; if he is thirsty, give him water to drink?* "In doing this you will heap burning coals on his head"* Romans 12:20

I had one more thought, and it was a question to God. What does this really mean to heap burning coals on his head? *After that I just said ok, I will do it.*

I began cutting the front lawn and nothing happened. I did keep looking at the front door expecting at any moment it would fly open and he would be in a rage, but it didn't happen so then I went through his backyard gate and started cutting his lawn. About halfway through it, he opened the door with a grimacing look on his face and he was shouting at me while the lawn mower was still on. I thought I heard him saying "You are crazy, you are crazy!"

I shut down the lawn mower and asked, "What did you say?" He repeated the words with the same look on his face, "You ARE CRAZY!!" His whole face was in a rage of anger. Then after what seemed like minutes passed with him and I starring at each other he said these most strange and amazing words in his French accent, "You Are Crazy Kind" and a slight smile poked through his face.

I said "Albert, I love you, man. I just wanted to help you." I asked him if I could proceed with cutting his grass and he said yes. As I finished the job he brought me a glass of water. We began to talk like old times but this time without the hate filled stories. When I look back on that day, I am certain of one thing, something changed in Albert's heart that day. I think back on how his face looked when he came out that back door and I remember the white-hot anger in his wrinkled face and then suddenly as we stood there in silence his face just melted, and a smile broke through. I think I now understand what the verse means when it says, "you will reap hot coals on his head" It means God will melt away the person's resistance to Him!

He Would Listen Intently

Not long after the lawn story Albert began calling my cell phone at work asking me to come over after I finished for the day. I was so glad he would invite me.

I would go over to his house and he would ask me questions about God and the bible but this time instead of "gotcha" questions, they were real heart questions and he never ended our conversation again waving his hand downward, saying "that's for you, not for me." The questions might have sounded similar to the prior questions he used to ask, but instead of scoffing he would listen intently. He asked me again the old question, "Why does God allow so much evil in the world if He was a good God?"

I told him life on earth was not meant to be this way. Life was meant to be like it was in the Garden of Eden where man and woman would walk with God in the cool of the evening and get to know Him and no sin was present. Unfortunately, man did sin, and God already had a plan to rescue him through His Son, Jesus Christ. His shed blood on the cross was God's punishment for our sins. Jesus did not stay dead but arose on the third day, and now leads us to the same victory if we turn away from our sins and receive His free gift of eternal life. This requires us letting go of our lives as we know them and, by faith, willing to follow Him throughout our lives. It is God's patience that allows Him to not kill everyone that causes someone else's pain. I finished by saying, "And that includes me and you, Albert. We both have been hurt but we both have hurt others. We would be dead now if God had decided to stop all the evil, because we both have done evil things."

Another day, Albert called me at work and said he was reading something and wanted to talk. I thought it might be the bible so I asked if it was and he said no, but it is some kind of spiritual book. The title he shared was strange so I said, "Albert, will you please get your bible and open it to the Book of Matthew and begin reading." To my shock he said, "I don't have a bible." He had maybe a thousand books in his library but no bible. So, I said to him, "You will have a bible this afternoon." It was such a privilege to go buy him a Bible and see him happy to get it. He told me later that he had begun to read it.

She and Others in the Community Had Been Praying For Albert

A week or so later I got a call from Rochelle, Albert's friend. She said she was about eighty and had been friends with Albert for quite some time. She tells me that she and her deceased husband had tried to be friends with him, but he had a falling out with her over something and he would hardly ever speak to her. She said, in fact, he would never walk his dog on their side of the street after the conflict. That came as no surprise, but she continued to tell me more than I had known about Albert, and we compared notes on what we each knew about Albert. Some things are still a mystery, but two themes ran true through everything we knew. He has always mistrusted people, and he is an angry man.

I shared with her that he and I had been having conversations about the Lord for over a year, and she was thrilled. In fact, she said she had been praying for Albert for years, and her Sunday school class has been praying for him as well. She said, "Tim, God sent you here to him. Don't give up." I could tell that she was such a wonderful lady with such a caring heart. She told me that she had picked him up in Atlanta from the airport at night among other countless things did for him, but he had not shown any real appreciation to her. She lastly said, "He trusts no woman." She said that she and others in the community had been praying for Albert for many years, and it was then that I realized that I was walking on the roads they helped pave over many years of their prayers for Albert, and I was just one of the pieces to Gods beautiful story of Him reaching out to Albert.

I began wondering if Albert might be warming up to the idea of going back to church with me so I thought I would test the waters and ask him if he would like to go with me the following Sunday. So, I asked him and to come to church, to my surprise, he said yes. The next Sunday he came back to church with me and he seemed to be pleased to be there and he seemed very comfortable being there. After church he had a pleasant conversation with Pastor Rod and on the way home, he said he enjoyed being there. Physically I noticed that He was moving slower, but he could still walk on his own with the help of a walking cane. I could tell that attending church and doing a lot of walking had exhausted him, so I asked him if I could stop and get him something to eat. I was hoping that he would want a real nutritious meal but instead he wanted just French fries from McDonalds. Since I began stopping from work and bringing him food he usually would default to fries only from McDonald's. But not just fries, more specifically, fries that had just been pulled out of the grease, and he wanted me to go in and make sure that what they put in the bag had just been removed from the deep fry grease. I wasn't about to mess that up because he being an Executive Chef meant he would have certainly sent me right back in until I get it right.

I started calling him on my way home from work each day, and because I could see that he was losing weight I would begin to name the different national foods like Italian, and Mexican, etc.. Just to see if I could get him to eat more. Sometimes it would work, and he would eat a descent amount, but other times it was back to the fries. We would sit and eat together and discuss some spiritual things he had thought about that day and I would head home.

I was getting concerned because we would have a good talk and he seemed to understand and desire the Lord so every now and then I would ask him if he was ready to make a decision to let Christ into his life and he would say not yet. One Sunday, my pastor was having the same concerns and said to him as he was leaving, "Albert, I know we are all going to die, and I may indeed die before you, but I am concerned that you will wait too long and your time be up." Albert pointed his finger at me and told him, "I will take this subject up with my spiritual attorney." Pastor Rod laughed and said, "I trust you are doing that but don't' wait too long." I, too, had the same concerns but until now nothing had moved the needle from "I am not ready yet." He even said to me, "You would not want me to make that decision unless I meant it, would you?" I said, honestly, "Of course not."

Three Days Crying Out To Jesus

In late July I had planned a weekend cruise with just my daughter Ellie and I. It was going to be a daddy-daughter adventure. She and I are a lot alike in that we love adventures, and over the years we have gone to the mountains, gone hiking through tunnels and waterfalls, gone camping in tents and down waterslides, not to mention what amounts to a safari right in Columbus, Georgia, where African animals poke their heads in your car as you ride through and they eat right out of your hands. Animals like giraffes, wildebeests, zebras, and water buffaloes. She has been amazing in her enthusiasm for everything God has made including sunrises, sunsets, and clouds. We have had a special relationship since she is the first child I was able to pour into spiritually while she was still young.

So I was looking forward to our next trip, but I was concerned about leaving Albert. He was still walking around on his own, but I was never sure when that may change. We got home late Sunday night and as I woke up early Monday morning, my phone rang. I had scheduled to be off from work that day so I could get everything cleaned up and ready for work. It was Albert and he asked if I could come over. I noticed concern in his voice, so I said, "I am coming now"

When I opened the front door the smell of poop almost knocked me down. I walked to the kitchen and as I got closer the smell got worse. When I rounded the corner Albert was sitting in the chair he always sat in while we talked and he begins telling me a story that

I can only repeat to you. I am not here to defend what he said or to validate it, or refute it, I am just going to be a witness of what I heard. If anyone ever wants me to do a lie detector test concerning this I will gladly do it, if you pay. I noticed a very large amount of poop on the carpet that looked like someone had tried to wipe it up and as I was about to gag, I asked Albert, "What happened?" He said, "I was walking into my kitchen and when I got to that door opening, someone shoved me hard to the floor and I landed in the corner against the cabinets." He said, "After I got up it shoved me again onto the floor here where the poop was."

I asked him, "Albert, was someone in your house?"

He said, "It was not someone. It was evil."

I asked, "Could you see it or them?"

He said, "No, but it was pure evil." He said, "I know you nor anyone will never believe me, but I don't care. I know what I am talking about. I am not crazy and I am telling you the truth." He said, "I could not get up after the second fall, so I laid there for three days crying out to Jesus to help me." He said, "I was finally able to pull the phone cord so that the phone fell on the floor next to me. I called Hughey to come get me up, and he did." He then said, "Tell me again how do I become a Christian?" I was completely floored hearing this story. I could not even think of another question to ask him because I was so stunned so I just regrouped and did what he asked me to do and I shared with him what we had talked about many times before and he said, "What you are telling me makes sense. I want to be a Christian."

I asked him if I could lead him in prayer and he said yes. I led him in prayer, and he asked Christ into his heart. When he had finished praying, he looked up at me and said I want to be baptized. Then he said, "Baptism doesn't save me, right?" I said, "Right," and explained what it meant to be baptized. That it was one of the first acts of obedience of a new believer in Christ and that it was a testimony to all who watch of what has happened in your heart. You have died to the old Albert and been buried in the grave symbolized by you being immersed under water, and through the Spirit of Christ, you are resurrected to walk in newness and freedom.

He said, "Will you baptize me?" "I said I am not the pastor but, I will be glad to assist him, and together we'll baptize you."

I embraced Albert with a hug and said, "Albert, I love you." And he said, "I love you too!"

After a short time, I headed home and told my roommate, Steven Santee, what just happened. I was crying, almost out of control, for joy. I had just watched a ninety-three-year-old man walk out of darkness into life. I called my brother Troy, and he and his son, Grayson, came over and we cleaned up all the poop. It was a joy to serve him, even though the joy did not make the smell any less, but soon it to be gone. Albert was BORN AGAIN! I felt like saying to everyone "I would like to announce the birth of a new citizen of God's kingdom and this new citizen Albert will live for an eternity in the presence of our savior Jesus Christ. His birth date is Tuesday, July 31st, 2018. His name is Adalbert Leslie Galicz.

How Albert looked the first years before his heart attack and his most loved painting

Whose Heart Was Like a Child

The next day Albert asked me if I would take him to the funeral home about a mile down the road. He wanted to make his funeral arrangements. We went down there and he quickly told the funeral home director that he wished to be cremated and his ashes placed in a container and told me he wanted his ashes spread in the woods of my choice. As, we were coming back he was tapping his chest with his hand and said in a very quiet voice, "I have peace in my heart," to which I said "Albert the Bible says that Jesus is the Prince of Peace." I am glad you shared that with me, and I am glad you sense His peace." He had such a calm about him that was quite unlike anything I had ever seen in him. He was restful, serene, and untroubled. We arrived back home, and I prayed with him a prayer of thanksgiving to God that he had rescued Albert. My voice broke at the thought that Albert would not suffer an eternity separated from God but instead, he would be firmly in God's hands and His presence and we would be together celebrating as brothers in Christ forever.

The following fifty-three days of Albert's life would be some of the most fulfilling moments I ever had, apart from my own experience and that of my family coming to know and follow Christ. There were so many daily surprises of Albert's life changing. I watched God transform a bitter, hate-filled man, into someone whose heart was like a child. He had a new gentleness that was in his voice and he was relaxed and peaceful. When I look back at this time, I almost scold myself and say, "Tim Padgett, what did you think was going to happen? Of course Albert was going to change." But I wasn't expecting it to be so dramatic. Don't get me wrong, I would still catch a glimpse of the old Albert on rare occasions, but what I mostly saw was a man being changed by the power of God into a new man that I was now getting to know all over again.

Toenail clipper

At work the next day, I got a call from Albert. He asked me to come over and I asked him what he was hungry for. I picked up his request, and we shared our hearts with each other as we did regularly. He asked if I would buy him a toenail clipper tomorrow on my way home from work. I assured him I would. When I came home that afternoon I gave it to him and then noticed he could hardly manage using it for two reasons. One was he was not flexible enough to bend over in order to reach his toes, and the second reason was his toenails were so thick that the big toenail clipper would not open up enough to get his toenail inside the clipping part. I was quickly in a mental struggle with the idea of me trying to cut his toenails because I had never cut anyone else's toenails except my children and I had never seen nails this long or this thick. They were more like a horse's hoof than a toenail. The second reason was because as I looked at his very large feet, they looked more like rough stone than flesh and it appeared that it may have been a while since they had been washed. I felt certain I had to do this, but I also felt a huge amount of reluctance to do it. I understand that there are multiple professions that this is what they do every day, but I had never thought about doing this for anyone else besides my children. Finally, I stopped all of my objections going on in my head by just saying to Albert, can I help do that for you? He agreed. What happened next, I was not prepared for and certainly had not thought of when I asked him. I proceeded to pull-up this small stool that was a perfect height for laying his foot on my lap and I began to chip away at what looked like a full year of toenail growth. They were not only long, but crusty and dirty. They looked like a science experiment gone bad. The full-size toenail clippers would not open wide enough to clip the thick nail, so I had to chip some on the top and then move to the bottom and do the same there. As I was clipping, I sense Christ speak to me through this verse of scripture as it comes to my mind, "Whatever you did for one of the least of these brothers and sisters of mine, you did it to me" *Matt. 25:40.* My eyes immediately filled up with tears. I could hardly see where to cut the nail next and I didn't want to wipe my tears and let Albert know I was crying because I thought he may not understand all that's happening right now. The next thought I had was "how I could have ever been given such a privilege like this?" I thought here I am holding the feet of Jesus in my hand as I minister to my new brother in Christ. I finally finish the job and Albert ask me if I would take the lotion he had and rub it on his feet. I really had no hesitation at this point, so I did as he asked began rubbing the lotion in as he just smiled with relief. I am sure it was soothing to his hard-crusty feet.

As I walked home that night, I weep for joy and thanked God for that humbling experience. When I look back on this event now, I can see that most of what happened that night was meant to change me. I can honestly say from this point on there was nothing too difficult that I was not willing to do. The only reason I would not do something for Albert was if I thought it might be unsafe. This would become the first of many similar but different episodes of caring for Albert and God using Albert to change me.

As the coming days clicked by, it was sadly becoming clear that just coming over in the afternoon would not be enough. I could see that Albert was not eating enough, so I tried to make sure he would get fed in the morning and afternoon. He was still walking on his own, but showed little interest in food. As I continued to do this he was eating less, so I asked him, "Albert, are you starving yourself on purpose or is it just that you have no appetite? Because if you are starving yourself, I will have no part of this and you will have to get someone else to do what I am doing." I said, "You have to try and eat more." He assured me he was not starving himself and would try to eat more, which he did. Each day I would pray with him and tell him I loved him, and he would say "I love you, too."

He Was Mad

A couple days later Albert asked if I would take him to an attorney so he could do his will. We made an appointment and when we sat down, the attorney began to ask all the standard questions and Albert answered each one. Then he got to the question of what he wanted to do with his house and other possessions like car, contents in his house, and the like. Albert turned to me and said, "Do you want my house?" Totally shocked I said, "Albert I cannot take your house." With a lot of back and forth with the attorney on that subject they both decided that Albert needed to come back again the next day in order to finalize the will and it be signed. When we go to the car and begin heading home Albert say's to me "It's my house, I can give it to whomever I want." He was not happy with me about not taking his house. I was so taken off guard by the whole conversation that I just said "Albert let me pray about this. I can't give you an answer today." He did not respond to that and just sat there silent the rest of the way home. When I walked into my house, I called my pastor because I had never had such a thing happen to me and I wanted to hear his advice. After he asked me many questions, he said "Tim, I see no reason why you shouldn't receive his gift." After he prayed for me and we hung up I just prayed and asked God to give me peace and guidance I needed to do what He would have me to do and I crawled into bed and went to sleep.

When I arrived at Albert's, he walked to the car and got in. It was clear he was mad, and I had not seen him mad or upset in any way since he asked Christ into his heart, so I asked him, "Albert, are you mad?" He said, with emphasis, "Yes, it is my house, and I want to give it to you and you won't take it."

I replied, "Albert, I don't want to argue with you. I am your ride today. I will sit back and wait for you and your attorney do all the talking and I will be quite."

When we sat down with the attorney, he asked Albert if he was okay, to which he replied "No, it is my house, and I want him to have it.

"The attorney said, "Well, if you want that, there is one way to make that happen today. I will fill out a quitclaim deed, and, upon your death, the house and all contents of your property will be Tim's." The attorney asked Albert if that is what he wanted to do, and Albert replied "yes". The attorney drafted the forms, Albert signed it, and it was done. Then Albert turned around and looked at me with a resolute face and almost seemed like he was taunting me, dipped his head and grinned. I had to get up and go to the bathroom because I was overwhelmed by emotion. I had tried unsuccessfully 6 times to buy a house, but God had not let that happen. He knew what He had planned to do. He didn't listen to my math when I prayed and explained to Him it was not wise of me to throw away rent money each year. He knew what His plans were. I only had one thought that would come to my mind. It would be this scripture, Matthew 6:33. *"Seek first the kingdom of God and His righteousness and all these things will be provided.*" He knew. He had done what Joel 2:25 says, *"I will restore the years that the locust has eaten away..."*

He knew. God did not owe me anything for the years I had plundered away. It was all my fault that I was where I was. It was none of His fault, yet He declares "I will restore the years." It was the beautiful picture of the prodigal son who had squandered away his father's inheritance, yet the father, again, put his royal robe and his royal ring on him and said to this broken and rebellious son who had come home, "remember who you are, You are my son." Did any of this happen because he deserved it? No. A million times, no. He (and I) deserved to be in despair and live without provision the rest of our lives, but that's not how the heart of God works.

I have read in the Bible of the great champions of faith who seemed to make no mistakes, and I have so much respect for them. As I have read deeper, however, I realized there are very few who rose to this level. What jumps out of the pages and into my mind, is that the bible is a record book of the great failures of men and women, and God's ability to raise us up and help us get back into the race He has given us to run. The bible is a record book of men's and women's dirty laundry including my own and God's ability to restore us from what has damaged us, and that should comfort all of us in a magnificent way. Christ gave his life for the broken. His very purpose is to rush to the side of the broken and we are all very broken people that desperately need to be intimately acquainted with this Savior. He alone can save us from our past and give us a brand new future.

As Albert finished up telling the attorney what he wanted to do with the rest of what he had and he named two things he wanted to do. He stated that he wanted his car to be sold and half of the proceeds to go to St. Jude's Children's Hospital and the other half to go to the South Dakota Children's Home for Native Indians. I thought this was so appropriate since he was an orphan, and he still had a huge place in his heart for orphans. The bible says in James 1:27: *"Pure and genuine religion in the sight of God the Father means caring for orphans and widows in their distress."*

The second thing Albert wanted to do was leave a gift to West Town Community Church, his own church in the end. He finished all the details and I started driving home. I could hardly speak because of what just happened. I usually am not short for words, but this overwhelmed me. All I could do is say to him, "Albert, you have blessed me and my entire family. I want to be a blessing to others as well. I cannot find the words to express what's going on in my heart right now, I love you Albert" and he said the same to me.

Church Erupted With Cheering

The following week the church made plans for a baptismal service that Albert and many others would be baptized. I would assist with Albert, and the excitement level in me was so high. What a privilege again to now be able to baptize this man who for three years had fought to not come to this point, and now he was pushing to participate. I asked my brother Troy if he saw a wheelchair while he was going to yard sales (something he loves and has become quite good at), would he pick it up.

He replied,"The last house just had one, and I will go right back there." Albert could have walked but it would have taken him multiple trips to the changing room, to and from the church and I knew he would be exhausted. So, as the time came, he and I changed our clothes and proceeded to the pool with Albert in the wheelchair. Pastor Rod and I baptized him, and the entire church erupted with cheering. The cheering completely caught me off guard. As I began to wheel him back to the room to change, many people came out of their seats and wrapped their arms around him. I would stop the wheelchair so they could speak, and these people were weeping their eyes out as they told him how grateful they were for him. He started weeping with them. It was the first time I had seen him cry, but it wouldn't be the last. They told him they loved him and how much this has had an influence on them. I couldn't hold back my own tears. I just watched as they uncontrollably loved on him. As we exited the back doors heading back to the dressing room to change it was just us two and we were crying out loud as I rolled him to the room. In there we both put our arms around each and embraced each other and cried.

He finally got his breath and said through the tears, "I have never seen love like this before." I will never forget those words as long as I live. I helped him get dressed and began to roll him out to the car, but I never got past the front doors where, once again, another group of people came to him one by one and expressed their love for him.

Afterwards we went out to eat at a restaurant and Albert became so tired he could not walk to the car so my son and brother held him up entirely and brought him to the car.

"Albert's Baptism"   *Ride home after Albert's baptism*

Albert and I walking into his home after baptism

Whole Story Complete

As the days passed; I could no longer get Albert to eat enough solid food. I remember thinking then he needs more help than I can give him each day. After asking around, Marie Cadden told me about Regency Hospice Care, and I called them and in just a small amount of time they were coming to his house and doing some wonderful things to help like bathing him, changing his sheets, and giving him something to drink or eat.

He would say, "I want milk!" Each day he would eat less and less. I shared that with hospice, and they said we can't make him eat, and he refused the offer of a nursing home. He said he wants to stay in his own home. So I just said I will keep doing anything that he will allow me to do to keep him eating.

One afternoon we were sitting at his table, and he was tapping his heart with his hand. Out of nowhere he said to me, "Tim, I have hated everyone all my life, but I hate no one now. All of my hate is gone."

Hearing those words made this whole story complete. I simply said to him, "God has removed your hate and replaced it with His love, Albert." He then said, "I wish I had made this decision a long, long time ago," to which I said, "If it makes you feel any better, I have never known a Christian that doesn't wish they had made the decision to follow Christ a lot sooner." I was watching his heart change right in front of me. His heart was being tenderized by the

Spirit of God in him, and I had a front row seat to see it. He never said another negative thing about anyone, his hurt heart was healed and he was at peace.

It's Your Fault

The next weeks were painful to watch, but there were still more wonderful moments as well. Albert's weight continued to drop and his strength as well. He was becoming less and less mobile as each day passed and had even fallen. I found him by his bed with no injuries, but he was unable to pick himself up. I got him into bed and ordered one of the Life Alert necklaces for him to wear. I also made him promise that he would not try to walk unless Hospice or myself were there. He agreed after some resistance, but he did not do a good job at keeping his word. He fell two more times. The ambulance came once, and the second time they called me first. When I arrived, I said, "Listen, Albert. If you want to stay here and want me to care for you, then here are the rules. Don't get out of the bed (he now had a hospital bed) unless you are using the portable toilet next to your bed. No walking on your own because I don't want to come some afternoon and see you laying on the floor with your head split open." He assured me he would not.

One early Saturday afternoon I decided to just go hang out with him and talk. I came in the house and as I turned to go down his hall he was naked and walking back to his room. I assume he had gone to the bathroom but I wasn't sure. I didn't yell because I was afraid that he would collapse before I got to him, so I just quietly walked up behind him and put my hands under his arm pits to hold him up. He was completely shocked I was there. I scolded him about walking around without assistance. I asked him how he could do this when he had given me his word. My lecture continued as I got him in bed, and he lifted his finger as to say "let me speak now," so I said, "What Albert?" He said "it's your fault!" To my total shock I said with my voice rising "*My* fault? How is this my fault?"

"Because you came over too early. If you had come at your regular time you would have never known."

I went from anger to bursting out laughing and he laughed too. All I could say is, "Albert, what am I going to do with you?" He still had his sense of humor. I told him, "I love you, my brother, but you are too much!" We continued to laugh!

He Wanted To Be At His New Address

By this time, Albert's health began going downhill. I asked Albert again if he would rather be in a nursing home with 24 hour help or even have someone spend the night in his house. He wanted no part of either of those ideas, so I told him after seeking advice from the hospice social worker and primary nurse that we would continue providing our help until it endangered him and that if he wanted that he would have to follow our advice closely or hospice would be forced to take action to have him committed to a nursing facility. He agreed and actually did what we asked. He now had to wear an adult diaper so that he did not have to get out of his bed and risk falling when he had to use the restroom.

What it meant for me and hospice would be daily sheet changes because he would leak through many times. I would change his shirt and diaper and wipe him down. One time after I had cleaned him after using the toilet, I lifted him up to put him back in the bed and he collapsed in my arms. He put his arms around me and pulled tightly, hugging me. I began patting my hand on his back and telling him "I love you, Albert," "We will get through this. It's going to be okay."

I had never walked down a path quite like this with either of my parents. Though my mom suffered and died from Alzheimer's, my dad was mostly with her daily until she had to be put in a nursing home. So I was learning on the job with Albert, and I was thankful that I could. It hurt to watch him decline, and I knew he was getting much closer to his death because now he refused solid food and only wanted milk three times a day and, of course, water.

One night when I was cleaning him up after coming home from work, he had lost almost all strength in his legs. His torso was as thin as the Jews in the Nazi concentration camps. I could count every rib. As Albert sat on the toilet, he was leaning his head on the bed as he did quite often, but this time he began shaking his head as if to be saying no. I asked him, "Albert, are you okay and do your need anything?" He mumbled, "No," still shaking his head.

I said, "What are your shaking your head for?"

"I want to go home!" he said.

I was shocked because up until this moment he had never been irrational about anything. I wondered if his mind was slipping and whether or not he was aware that he was indeed home in his house. So I said, "Albert, you are home. You are in your house."

Albert continued shaking his head, then pointed one finger up toward heaven and said again, "I want to go home."

I said "Albert, do you mean you want to go home to heaven?"

He said "Yes, yes! I want to go home to heaven."

I knew now he was so certain of where his home was, and it wasn't 2139 Balfour Street, Augusta, Georgia. He knew his time was getting close, and he wanted to be at his new address. He wanted out of the 93-year-old earth suit that was causing him great pain and discomfort, and into his last heavenly suit that would never be in pain again. He was ready to go. So I tried to comfort him by saying, "Albert, it won't be long. We will get through this." I hugged him and told him again that I loved him and put him to bed. It was obvious things were changing fast, and hospice had to give him morphine tablets because of the pain he was in due to his heart continuing to fail.

September 9th

I had some things on my mind that I wanted to share with Albert, but I did not want to wait too long. I got my chance on September 9, 2018 when I was over at his house doing the normal cleaning and talking to Albert. He seemed to be very alert and talkative, so I decided the timing was right. I sat down by his bed and said, "Albert, there are some things I have been wanting to share with you that you do not know."

He said, "Okay, go ahead."

"First, I thank you, Albert for how you have given me new faith. I have seen in you someone in his old age who was so opposed to God and others, turn and repent of his sins. I can now see people with hard hearts with a new hope and not with doubt and hopelessness as I did in the past. This is because of you."

"Second," I continued, "I have shared your story now with countless numbers of people, and I will continue to share it after you are gone."

My hope is that someone will walk up to him in heaven and introduce themselves and say to him, "My name is Tom, and I want you to know, Albert, I heard your story of God's mercy, grace, and forgiveness, and your story gave me hope that if God did that for you, He could do that for me, as well. I gave my life to Christ, too!" "Third, I am going to write a book about your life because others are encouraging me to, and I feel impressed to do it. I told him that I believe God will use this hopefully in many people's lives and that I love you dearly my brother.

Then I asked Albert this question, "Albert, what would you like the title of the book to be?" And he says to me after some thought, "Hope Saved Me" Then he asked me in his wonderful french accent, "Is it good?" I said to him, yes that is very good.

Albert reached for my hand, and as we grasped each other's hand, we began to weep together. It was a weeping that I had never shared with anyone. It was joyous because of where he was now spiritually.

Imaginings of the Future He Wouldn't Have

He was at peace. He was filled with love and changed. But it was also a weeping of sadness that our time together was almost up. I wondered if he had been around for three to five more years, what would those years have looked like? Would he have gone back and tried to make right the relationships with neighbors and family members? Would I have seen him become a great testimony to others? My imaginings of the future he wouldn't have were many, but God's plans are even better. As we held hands, I said again, "Albert, I love you." He said the same to me.

That night, each time I tried to get up to leave he grabbed my hand more firmly. His breathing was heavy, and I think he may have been having some heart issue, but he said he was okay. I sat with him in silence for about an hour more holding his hand, and then he released my hand. I prayed for him and walked home. The rest of this week was normal, but Albert was extremely tired and was in and out of sleeping preventing us from talking much.

Nursing Home or Face Legal Issues

The following Sunday, after visiting with Albert, I went to bed and I was nauseated and restless the entire night. I called in sick on Monday and went to check on Albert and give Him his milk and water.

I found Albert sideways in the bed. He was covered from head to toe with poop. I knew I could not handle the job by myself, so I straightened him up in the bed and called hospice for help. The nurse arrived and was concerned. I offered to help but explained that I may have to run outside if I became overwhelmed since I was already nauseated. We worked for over an hour, but got him clean and back in the bed.

The hospice social worker came over and broke the news to Albert that she now had to send him to a nursing home or face legal issues if she did not. She explained that it is called self-negligence if he could not manage himself. The ambulance came and transported him within hours.

I went to visit each day, but Albert was completely unaware that I was there. Something had happened to him medically and he could no longer drink without choking violently. On Wednesday, his doctor told me he probably would not last but a few days longer.

Just In The Nick Of Time

Early the following Saturday morning, I received a call that Albert was not breathing and had no heartbeat. They could not announce his death – only the coroner can do that. I rushed to the nursing home and found him in his room. They told me to take as much time as I wanted. I opened the door and Albert was lying on his bed. I knelt beside him and prayed, "Father, thank you that Albert is home with you. Thank you, Father, that you saved him just in the nick of time." I could not help but kept repeating to the Lord, "Just in the nick of time," with tears of joy and sadness. I thanked God for the short time on earth he was a believer and I prayed that God would use Albert's life more after his death, much like the thief on the cross who was saved just in the nick of time. I prayed, "Lord, I will miss him, but I will see him soon. Thank you for my friend and my brother."

As I sat in the room by his bed, so many things were going through my mind. I felt at peace and I just wanted to sit a little longer as I had done so many times at his house. The thoughts of his words that night weeks ago came to mind, "I want to go home." And now he was home. It was just as I had told him, "It won't be long."

Our church had a memorial service for Albert. I brought some of his paintings and gave them to anyone who wanted one. Of course, some of the people who had been involved with Albert took one like the hospice social worker who said they hung it on the wall of their office to remember Albert. It was a good time of reflecting on his life and the change that had happened.

Several weeks had gone by and I had to decide where to spread Albert's ashes. It occurred to me that our men's retreat was coming up later in the fall and what better location than on Folly Beach Island where our men's group had so many wonderful memories in times past. So, one afternoon a group of us men gathered, and we spread his ashes in the small, wooded area next to the retreat house and celebrated Albert's life and what he had meant to each of us. What I never thought about at this time was that a little over 2 years later I would be speaking to our men and their son's and telling Albert's story for the very first time. Many of them had no idea until I shared with them that his burial location was right outside our house. It was a beautiful moment for me to be able to share with these men who had meant so much to me and to visit that location again and reflect on how much Albert had meant to me personally and how God had used him to change my life.

93-Year-Old Frenchman

It was now time to move out of my rental house and move into Albert's home. Some things I found made me laugh, like the sign I found hanging on his fence that read "Don't poison my trees. I will be taking soil samples and sending them to the lab for test. I will prosecute anyone who is guilty." There were the plastic grocery bags he collected that would fill an entire outside garbage can and they were all brand new. He must have asked every place he stopped if he could have some. It seems he took many as they would give. Then there were the blankets the airlines will give you when you are chilled except these were all still in plastic packaging and had never been opened. I found stockpiles of food in storage bins that had expired years ago. Albert saved it all, just in case.

As I began to take care of certain things as executor of his will, I began to run into a repeating story. While I was at one of businesses closing his account, the first lady asked if she could help me. I explained that I was Albert's executor and I needed to close his account. She said, "Okay, are you one of his family members?"

I answered, "No, I was his neighbor."

She asked how I became the executor. She was more curious than nosy because a neighbor is probably an odd choice for executor.

I told her he was 93 and had a lot of broken relationships, so he had asked me. She continued to ask more questions, so I said, "I will just share a quick version of Albert's story." I shared how he had hated everyone and lived his life so broken and that he asked Christ into his heart and everything had changed for him. I shared how we became so close in our friendship as new brothers in Christ and that He became a loving and kind man in his last days. She said, "that is amazing, it is about to make me cry". She could not finish the transaction without help from her supervisor so she called her to come help. As her supervisor started to help me, she began to ask the same questions. Once again I was sharing about Albert's conversion to Christ, and once again she shared that she was so moved by this story.

After this I had a meeting later that day with one more person in order to wrap up Albert's affairs. The lady that helped me began to ask me many questions about Albert and our relationship. She was very drawn to the story and continue to ask me many other questions about him. Finally, she stopped what she was doing and turned to me and said, "I can't hold back my tears at hearing this story." She said, "You need to write a book about his life". When I came home, I told my roommate Steven what had happened, and he was as amazed as I was. Others began to tell me they had shared his story with many people as did my Pastor. He shared that he met with a group of pastors and shared with them different stories about Albert, and they asked permission to share it with their congregations. My pastor also encouraged me to think about writing a book about all the things that had happened.

When I told others Albert's story, many would say, "You need to write a book about this." I began to realize that Albert's story was giving people hope. I alone have shared Albert's story with hundreds of people, and I have no idea how many it's been shared with by others. The message of hope is being carried and told.

When I began writing this book there were two things that I prayed for and desired that God would do in each person that reads this book. The first thing I prayed for was any Christian that has experienced what it means to become a shipwreck like me, and they have lost all hope of ever returning to that relationship with God they once had. I prayed that this would give them the courage to say enough is enough. I prayed that they would get up and run back to the heavenly Father and begin a new journey with Him. I ask that you turn to God now and say, "I will do anything you ask of me; I ask forgiveness of all my sins. I will now follow you and finish this race that I started months or years ago."

Secondly, I prayed that God would use Albert's story to give every person hope. Even if you think you are the worst person on this planet earth. I pray that Albert's story has shown clearly that if God can put up with a 93-year-old Frenchman that hated everyone, that surely, He can do for you what He did for Albert. If you do not know what it means to have a relationship with Christ, will you ask Him into your heart now? He is knocking on your heart's door and saying, "If you open the door, I will come in and forgive you of all your sins." God loves you so much that He gave his Son to die for your sins and my sins. He has paid the price through His death for our sins that we could never pay. I pray you will trust Him now.

Made in the USA
Columbia, SC
22 September 2024

42078075R00061